WHAT IS YOUR LOCUST

The Key to Defeating Darkness

"The Lord shall fight for you, and ye shall hold your peace." (KJV) Exodus 14:14

Unless otherwise indicated, all Scriptures quotations are taken from the King James Version (KJV), ©1986 by Barbour and Company, Inc. Published by World Bible Publishers; Iowa Falls, IA 50126.

Scriptures notations marked (KJV) are taken from the KJV Version of the Bible.

"What Is Your Locust? The Key to Defeating Darkness"

Printed in the United States of America
Amazon ISBN: 9781976974137
©February 2018 by:
D'Anointed Heart Publishing

D'Anointed Heart Publishing
 #512
40 Cypress Creek Parkway,
Houston, TX 77090.

"The Lord shall fight for you, and ye shall hold your peace." (KJV) Exodus 14:14

Cover design by: Brianniah Tranthum

Table of Contents

"The Lord shall fight for you, and ye shall hold your peace." (KJV) Exodus 14:14

"The Lord shall fight for you, and ye shall hold your peace." (KJV) Exodus 14:14

Introduction

Exodus 14:14 teaches us that the battles we engage in are not ours; they are the Lord's, and as such, we must keep our peace. Despite this wise teaching from Moses, however, we let ourselves become frustrated and overwhelmed by chaos and confusion.

The Bible makes it clear that it is only when we surrender our battles to the Lord that we will triumph over them. Some of us insist on doing things our own way, yet blame God when things go awry.

"The Lord shall fight for you, and ye shall hold your peace." (KJV) Exodus 14:14

We assume too many challenges that hold or have held us in bondage; chained, shackled, *trapped.* These challenges become our locusts. Serpents then become a part of our territory.

Even though God has used me as His Vessel to write His Word, I have, perhaps against that same Word, allowed myself to be held in bondage by: toxic relationships, alcohol, depression, night clubs, pride, and selfishness.

"The Lord shall fight for you, and ye shall hold your peace." (KJV) Exodus 14:14

It was not easy to rid myself of these locusts. It was only through the Power of my Lord and Savior Jesus Christ that I was able to do so.

What locusts and serpents are you struggling with and facing today? What behaviors, decisions, and/or daily living patterns are opening the door for serpents to enter your life and defile your flesh?

Locusts come to devour, leaving nothing in their wake; serpents come to torment, poison and subdue us.

"The Lord shall fight for you, and ye shall hold your peace." (KJV) Exodus 14:14

Drugs, depression, sexual perversions, pride, greed, and wrath are but a few examples of the multitude of sins we encounter and battle daily. It is sins such as these that open the gateway for locusts and serpents to enter our lives and spirits. I want you to understand and appreciate that we simply cannot eradicate them on our own.

Without God's Divine Protection, those and all other sins will become thorns which cement themselves in our families, relationships, finances, physical appearances, and most importantly, our hearts.

"The Lord shall fight for you, and ye shall hold your peace." (KJV) Exodus 14:14

The key question is: are you ready to surrender your battles to Jesus Christ? It bears repeating that the battles we engage in are not ours; they are the Lord's!

Take the time to pray to God every single daily. Ask God for strength, and for anything else you may need.

"The Lord shall fight for you, and ye shall hold your peace." (KJV) Exodus 14:14

Chapter 1: About the Locust

Exodus 10:15

"For they covered the face of the whole earth, so that the land was darkened; and they did eat every herb of the land, and all the fruit of the trees which the hail had left: and there remained not any green thing in the trees, or in the herbs of the field..."

Locusts infest and cause destruction everywhere they roam. Historically, the natural disasters locusts caused were feared. These disasters required substantial rebuilding and restoration efforts because the sheer damage the locusts inflicted.

"The Lord shall fight for you, and ye shall hold your peace." (KJV) Exodus 14:14

This may sound horrifying, but I have good news: God wants to rebuild and restore your garden by destroying all the locusts which lay within it. For your information: locusts swarm rapidly and in great numbers. Therefore, they can cover great distances while attacking and destroying crops and vegetation.

In fact, a single locust can consume large amounts of crops and vegetables daily. Their collective impact causes major destruction, which may lead to misery, poverty and starvation.

"The Lord shall fight for you, and ye shall hold your peace." (KJV) Exodus 14:14

Once locusts destroy crops and vegetation, significant nurturing is needed to revert those crops and vegetation to an ordinary and healthy state.

There can be no doubt that locusts are destructive, but they know not the capacity of the harm they cause. They are not aware or mindful of whose crops or vegetation they destroy. Locusts are insects, and insects do what comes naturally or instinctually to them. I have come to the realization locusts are only the beginning, if that.

"The Lord shall fight for you, and ye shall hold your peace." (KJV) Exodus 14:14

Depending on the nature of our decisions and behavior, we may inadvertently be opening the door for multiple serpents to enter our lives and spirits. Our problems are like our very own locusts: if left unresolved, they will devour us, and their thorns will get thicker, sturdier, and more painful to bear.

Deuteronomy 28:42
"All thy trees and fruit of thy land shall the locust consume."

The day eventually came where I was tired of being devoured by locusts.

"The Lord shall fight for you, and ye shall hold your peace." (KJV) Exodus 14:14

"The Lord shall fight for you, and ye shall hold your peace." (KJV) Exodus 14:14

One day, as I was praying to the Lord, I asked myself, *"Yneka, what locusts and serpents have caused you to be so lost, confused, and tired?"* My answers were as follows: depression; toxic relationships; rejection; alcohol; partying at night clubs; temptation; the absence of my children's fathers in my children's lives, and a personal lack of direction for my own life.

These things were the locusts which invaded my territory and compromised my well – being.

"The Lord shall fight for you, and ye shall hold your peace." (KJV) Exodus 14:14

Personal Reflection:

Having read the first chapter, do you now understand the primary purpose of locusts?

Which locusts are currently devouring you?

How long have you been trying to combat your locusts on your own?

Reflect on, then write a list of, the damage the locusts' swarm has caused in your life and in your heart.

Once again: take the time to pray to God. Ask Him for strength, and for anything else you may need.

> *"The Lord shall fight for you, and ye shall hold your peace."* (KJV) Exodus 14:14

Chapter 2: Give Your Locusts Over to Christ

The Bible is the inerrant Word of God; it is our truth, our double – edged sword, our beginning and end; it is our salvation, and it provides us with clear instructions on how to be saved.

There are Scriptures for every locust that exists, but we must be willing to not only hear God's Instructions through those Scriptures, but to apply them to our lives.

"The Lord shall fight for you, and ye shall hold your peace." (KJV) Exodus 14:14

The Word of God always prevails, and its authority is buttressed by wisdom and knowledge from the tree of goodness.

Proverbs 2:6

"For the Lord gives wisdom; From His mouth come knowledge and understanding."

Locusts serve only one purpose; to demolish the crops and vegetation of our gardens, thereby decreasing our faith and interrupting God's Perfect Will from infiltrating our lives. Each of us became a great work from the time God created us.

"The Lord shall fight for you, and ye shall hold your peace." (KJV) Exodus 14:14

Locusts serve to diminish our faith and love in God while increasing our work load. Our thoughts change because that which locusts devour always takes extra work to restore. It is often the case where locusts are extraordinarily aggressive in their attacks, and where serpents invade our personal space; when this happens, it is enough to conjure feelings of hopelessness. Fear not, however, for there IS hope, and you CAN overcome ALL your obstacles!

"The Lord shall fight for you, and ye shall hold your peace." (KJV) Exodus 14:14

This is a fact, because our God is a God of resurrection who patiently waits for us to return to Him: our first love. No attack from satan can ever take place without God's permission. God tests our faith and decision - making capabilities, just as was the case when God permitted satan to test Job's faith.

Locusts may have their own sense of direction, but they cannot destroy as they want to do without our help. Think about it: for locusts to destroy crops and vegetation, there must be crops, and vegetation present to be tempted by.

"The Lord shall fight for you, and ye shall hold your peace." (KJV) Exodus 14:14

God may provide us with His Word and a proper sense of direction, but He already knows when we are going to rebel and ignore His directions. Our rebellion in turn grants locusts more and greater opportunities to ruin that which we hold dear. With that in mind, we have no choice but to surrender our locusts over to Christ and allow Him to fight our battles as we remain in peace.

God, in His Omniscience, knows the precise day and hour at which the locusts will attack whenever we are caught off – guard.

"The Lord shall fight for you, and ye shall hold your peace." (KJV) Exodus 14:14

Therefore, the enemy is always anxious to increase the number of locusts for his attack against you, which results in the attack being more severe. The enemy is anxious and impatient just like us; he stands ready to kill, steal and destroy at a moment's notice.

Proverbs 30:27

"The locusts have no king, yet they all advance in ranks."

Are locusts also not eager and willing to kill, steal and destroy? Do we appreciate

"The Lord shall fight for you, and ye shall hold your peace." (KJV) Exodus 14:14

that locusts will ensnare the Power of Christ to secure their own victory over our lives?

Are the locusts of alcohol, depression, drugs, temptation, and pride devouring your life and the lives of your family members?

I guarantee you that the first part of our problems is that we tend to devise our own solutions. When we do this, we damn ourselves to the serpents' pit. This is when serpents crawl about our flesh and bind us, which makes us feel like there is no way out. God's Word, Knowledge, and Wisdom

"The Lord shall fight for you, and ye shall hold your peace." (KJV) Exodus 14:14

provide the ultimate escape, no matter how many locusts abound. God's Truth is the single best solution to our problems.

God's Plan and Will over our lives is always bigger and greater than we can possibly imagine, because it is for His Glory.

Jeremiah 29:11

"For I know the thoughts I think towards you, says the Lord, thoughts of peace and not of evil, to give you a future and a hope."

Whenever the locusts of alcohol, drugs, depression, pride, and temptation

successfully attack us, our faith falls into the hands of the enemy. Meanwhile, serpents

"The Lord shall fight for you, and ye shall hold your peace." (KJV) Exodus 14:14

have been lying in wait, watching patiently, eyes alert and tongues flickering, leaving no room for peace.

With the evil forces of the locust and the serpent combined, everything good is consumed, filled with darkness, and broken into immeasurable pieces. This process, begins with *us*. We worry over every little thing. Our thoughts become impure and replete with anger and confusion, and our hearts no longer shine bright with God's Love.

"The Lord shall fight for you, and ye shall hold your peace." (KJV) Exodus 14:14

Some of us are continually plagued by locusts, serpents and darkness. If you are one of those people, I have awesome news for you: God will restore everything which the enemy has stolen from us.

We must first, however, allow our hearts to be open and willing to receive Jesus Christ Himself. We must be prepared to truly process God's Word in our hearts and spirits before we can prevail over the darkness. Once we have done these things, the light within us will be restored; this is God's Plan and Purpose for those who love and worship

"The Lord shall fight for you, and ye shall hold your peace." (KJV) Exodus 14:14

Him.   While we rebuild, we must learn, derive wisdom from and apply God's Word to our lives, and in so doing, surrendering our locusts, darkness and serpents to God.

My testimony (Part 1)

God intended for me to write this book and use it to share my own testimony, which may very well be able to help someone else with their own struggles. One thing about this testimony of mine is that I smiled as I

"The Lord shall fight for you, and ye shall hold your peace." (KJV) Exodus 14:14

wrote about it, the pain of my remembrance of its surrounding events notwithstanding.

As of today, the 18th December 2017, I have been married for 1 year and 7 months. One day a few weeks ago, I made a post on social media stating, *"I'd rather be single."*

I also changed my status from 'married' to 'single.' This change reflected how I felt; I'd lost my faith, and I knew I was done with my marriage irrespective of how much I loved my husband. I can recall telling him that the things we were going through

"The Lord shall fight for you, and ye shall hold your peace." (KJV) Exodus 14:14

would either be our testimony, or my testimony.

My locusts manifested themselves in thoughts of drinking, going to party at night clubs, and experiencing another bout of depression. The enemy even invaded my flesh with feelings of lust.

"The Lord shall fight for you, and ye shall hold your peace." (KJV) Exodus 14:14

My husband and I constantly fought about our finances, the way he disciplined our children, the infrequency with which he studied God's Word, when and what time we did certain things, the fact that I spoke to everyone in my life except him, and his own locusts and serpents. My husband also tried to hold me by force during those times when I wanted to be left alone.

His locusts and serpents, combined with my own, swarmed and crawled their way into our marriage, creating darkness and negative space between us.

"The Lord shall fight for you, and ye shall hold your peace." (KJV) Exodus 14:14

Finally, one day, I read, accepted and declared the Scripture of Exodus 14:14. The locusts, serpents, darkness and space gradually decreased afterwards. This time was not an easy time for either us; it was a consistent and daily struggle. We both had to learn how to fight to do and continue doing what was right for the sake of the marriage God Blessed us with. I refused to allow my serpents and locusts lay claim to our marriage, but my husband and I, at the time, were not equally yoked in terms of our resolve in that regard.

"The Lord shall fight for you, and ye shall hold your peace." (KJV) Exodus 14:14

While I knew that the reclamation of our marriage would require us to temporarily separate from one another, my husband was as blind as he was inattentive. We both knew neither of us would ever be the same if we allowed our locusts and serpents to tear our marriage asunder. This is because each journey a Christian embarks on teaches, disciplines, and makes her/him stronger.

"The Lord shall fight for you, and ye shall hold your peace." (KJV) Exodus 14:14

God provided me with clear instructions. While following those instructions, I often read through the first book God granted me permission to write: "The Journal of Truth and The Beginning."

This book comprised of the locusts and serpents I needed to battle to remain in my marriage, together with the soldiers God prepared to help me reach the other side of my trials and tribulations. The book also included God's instructions and wisdom.

"The Lord shall fight for you, and ye shall hold your peace." (KJV) Exodus 14:14

I am confident that God's instructions not only applied to me, but to those who read that book and needed them for themselves.

Presently, my husband and I still experience hardships, but we consistently remind ourselves of God's Love and Truth. Our marriage is no different when it comes to God restoring and rebuilding the new from the old, making us perfect in unity. We must always remember that all things are possible through Christ who strengthens us, as it is written and declared in Philippians 4:13.

"The Lord shall fight for you, and ye shall hold your peace." (KJV) Exodus 14:14

Personal Reflection:

After reading chapter 2, are you willing to be honest and forthcoming about the locusts which have been devouring you?

Ask yourself: are you tired of your good fruits being repeatedly destroyed?

Make a list of people your locusts have caused you to lose and/or hurt.

Ask yourself: what do you have to lose in submitting your locusts to Jesus Christ?

"The Lord shall fight for you, and ye shall hold your peace." (KJV) Exodus 14:14

Take the time to pray and speak to God. Everything you say will be between you and Him. Trust God with your weaknesses and ask Him to give you the strength to surrender your locusts over to Him.

"The Lord shall fight for you, and ye shall hold your peace." (KJV) Exodus 14:14

Chapter 3: Faith Is a Winner

Locusts are a part of our lives because of the world we live in, and the events that are occurring nowadays. The problem is that we open our doors and allow locusts to swarm inside until we are partially or completely devoured by them. For some, this means giving in to the locusts and not having enough faith and trust in God to secure victory over them. How often we forget that the Scripture of Matthew 17:20, which says that one of the keys to achieving victory

"The Lord shall fight for you, and ye shall hold your peace." (KJV) Exodus 14:14

through Christ is having faith the size of a mustard seed.

Hebrews 11:1

"Now faith is the substance of things hoped for, the evidence of things not seen."

Even though it may seem like thousands of locusts are surrounding you, it is imperative that you walk by faith, and not by sight. Place your trust and confidence in Jesus Christ, our Lord and Savior. God created Heaven and Earth and all the living creatures therein, including locusts. God,

"The Lord shall fight for you, and ye shall hold your peace." (KJV) Exodus 14:14

therefore, achieves victory over the locusts

who plague His Earth by default!

"The Lord shall fight for you, and ye shall hold your peace." (KJV) Exodus 14:14

Locusts may devour crops and vegetation with coordinated stealth, but when we give God our problems, locusts' victory over our lives is never an option. Now, just because we surrender our locusts to God, does not mean that things will be easy and unproblematic for us going forward.

Locusts are energized by guilt, shame, grief, resentment and anger. We must overcome them and all other manifestations of sin with the Blood of Jesus Christ.

"The Lord shall fight for you, and ye shall hold your peace." (KJV) Exodus 14:14

God did not create us to endure relentless pain; He created us to be warriors who enter and do battle in accordance with His Word and Truth.

John 8:32

"And ye shall know the truth, and the truth shall make you free."

God allows us to journey through Earth's wilderness, so that we may return to Him: our first love. We gain spiritual maturity and wisdom through this journey.

"The Lord shall fight for you, and ye shall hold your peace." (KJV) Exodus 14:14

Faith is the ultimate victor, because no matter what the number, size or speed of the locusts, our God is a God of freedom and healing.

Having faith is an indication of the fact that we trust in none other but God. We trust in God to ordain our steps and intercede on our behalf. God's Spirit offers great discernment and wisdom to all open hearts and ears.

Proverbs 1:7

"The fear of the Lord is the beginning of knowledge: but fools despise wisdom and instruction."

"The Lord shall fight for you, and ye shall hold your peace." (KJV) Exodus 14:14

When the locusts of alcohol, drugs, temptation, depression, hate, rebellion and pride swarm us, we become weak and helpless unless we adorn the full armor of God's Word and Truth, which, combined with our faith in him, all work in tandem with one another. We achieve victory against locusts, serpents and all other forces of destruction; God created them all, so when the time is right, *he will destroy them.*

Many of us invite locusts into our lives even after God has destroyed them outright or provided a way of escape from them.

"The Lord shall fight for you, and ye shall hold your peace." (KJV) Exodus 14:14

How can we escape the locust when we continuously invite its presence? How can we escape the serpents when we allow them to return to their territory (or we return to theirs) time and again?

It is often the case that when we make the ill – fated decision to return, the destruction, chaos and confusion we experience increases because we bring *more* for those forces to act upon. The enemy wants to kill, steal and destroy because that is his purpose; it is his plan of revenge against God.

"The Lord shall fight for you, and ye shall hold your peace." (KJV) Exodus 14:14

These temporary things that feel good are locusts devouring our crops and vegetation, combined with serpents poisoning our flesh. *It is by faith and trusting in the Lord, our heavenly Messiah,* **that we achieve victory over all those things because we** *"Trust in the Lord with all thine heart; and lean not unto thine own understanding."* (Proverbs 3:5).

To 'lean not unto thine own understanding' is to entirely surrender our lives to God, thereby trusting Him and His Perfect Plan for our lives.

"The Lord shall fight for you, and ye shall hold your peace." (KJV) Exodus 14:14

In due season and by way of the execution of God's Plan, all locusts and serpents will flee in Jesus' name. Our God is a patient God, and He will always accept us. Nothing that is not of God will follow him or prevail against Him. For as long as we repose confidence in God and be servient to Him, He will never leave or forsake us.

Faith is having confidence in ourselves and God that we will overcome all the obstacles in our lives. We must never forget that our God is a God of healing, deliverance and restoration. This Scripture says:

> *"The Lord shall fight for you, and ye shall hold your peace."* (KJV) Exodus 14:14

"For God so loved the world, that he gave his only begotten Son, that whosoever believeth in him should not perish, but have everlasting life. " (John 3:16). Take note that God did not specify persons of any name, gender, race sexuality, class or any other distinction.

We as human beings tend to pay attention to the number, size and speed of our locusts, which causes us to lose focus on the Power of Christ and His Ways. We do not handle or process situations as Christ does.

"The Lord shall fight for you, and ye shall hold your peace." (KJV) Exodus 14:14

Without the Power of Christ to compel us, our thoughts become our own, our decisions become unwise and misdirected, and our ways become enveloped with selfishness. Instead, we are to rest easy, having faith in God, knowing that He is at work.

Neither locusts and serpents care whether we observe them; yet they crave and thrive off our undivided attention. They care not for our environment, and as such, they will do and think as they like. The question is: what do we think about all this, and what will we do about it?

"The Lord shall fight for you, and ye shall hold your peace." (KJV) Exodus 14:14

Will we remain steadfast in our faith, or will we capitulate and die? When a person has an intimate and sincere love for God, we seek His Solutions, not those conjured by humans. When humans grow weary, God stands firm; He watches, warns us, and discerns our spirits.

Titus 1:2

"In hope of eternal life, which God, that cannot lie, promised before the world began."

Our God is eternal. He does not rest or become ill or tired. Where, then, will we

"The Lord shall fight for you, and ye shall hold your peace." (KJV) Exodus 14:14

place our faith: in the temporary nature of human kind, or the permanence of God?

The answer is clear: our God sustains forever, is a God of faith, and is our victor.

Personal Reflection:

Take just a few minutes of quiet time and solitude. Isolate yourself from all possible distractions. Speak to God about your faith. What did He say to you in response?

*Do you believe in earnest that **faith** is a winner?*

"The Lord shall fight for you, and ye shall hold your peace." (KJV) Exodus 14:14

In which areas of your life do you find that your faith is lacking?

What instructions have God given you that will increase your **faith**? Are you able and willing to obey God's Instructions?

Take the time to pray, asking God to increase your **faith** in the areas of your life in which it is lacking, and in those areas where you need it the most.

"The Lord shall fight for you, and ye shall hold your peace." (KJV) Exodus 14:14

Chapter 4: Hindering the Power of The Holy Spirit

The truth is this: locusts hinder the Power of the Holy Spirit simply because we allow them to. What's more, God is going to complete His Work even in the face of those hindrances or in circumstances where we cannot or do not work for ourselves.

My testimony (Part 2)

I allowed a man to devour me once; our situation placed me in bondage. At the time, my life was severely out of order.

> *"The Lord shall fight for you, and ye shall hold your peace."* (KJV) Exodus 14:14

I was experiencing hardships with school; I recently exited a sour relationship; I purchased a new home; I ran a marathon with my son because of his special needs, and I was working full time while juggling all these responsibilities. My flesh was too weak to stand firm and let go of the things that, in retrospect, were only temporary solutions to my problems. I constantly fantasized about all the fun my relationship partner and I would have. I was enraged because I did not receive everything I wanted out of the relationship.

"The Lord shall fight for you, and ye shall hold your peace." (KJV) Exodus 14:14

My depression consequently worsened. I felt like I was not good enough, even though I was trying my best. I increased my consumption of alcohol; my intention was to drown out my feelings, pain, thoughts, and inner chaos. I carried my pride on my shoulder since I wanted to do things my way.

The effect of my temptations on me was severe, because I believed I could not live without my relationship partner. Drugs became a part of my routine. I felt like I could not handle living life any longer, so I wanted to commit suicide.

"The Lord shall fight for you, and ye shall hold your peace." (KJV) Exodus 14:14

My relationship partner, my job and my children were my only sources of joy... or so I thought. I prayed to God and asked Him to fix a relationship that should have never existed to begin with. I allowed this one man and my chaotic schedule to bring a plethora of locusts and serpents into my life. Locusts devoured my flesh, mind, heart and thoughts on an almost daily basis. Serpents slithered around intensely in my spirit. My crops and vegetation were bitter and dry.

We are God's vessels, and we belong to the ***Body of Christ.***

"The Lord shall fight for you, and ye shall hold your peace." (KJV) Exodus 14:14

God has granted us the ability to bear good and faithful fruits. Our fruits are our children, finances, spouses, and God's Purpose for us; that is, the ministry He calls us to. There are many still living among the darkness, who are being devoured, and whose spiritual gifts and talents are being hindered.

Locusts are swarming and devouring everything and everyone we love. It is the vessel that belongs to Christ which allows them to swarm and the serpents to slither that are responsible for what they do.

"The Lord shall fight for you, and ye shall hold your peace." (KJV) Exodus 14:14

I am no different from you; I have been guilty as well, and on far more than one occasion. When we are unprepared to submit to Christ, we are rebelling against, resisting, ignoring, and hindering the **Power of the Holy Spirit.** We must also safeguard ourselves against the teachings of false prophets.

1 John 4:1

"Beloved, believe not every spirit, but try the spirits whether they are of God: because many false prophets are gone out into the world."

"The Lord shall fight for you, and ye shall hold your peace." (KJV) Exodus 14:14

Some of us seem to forget that our God is a grieving and jealous God.

Nevertheless, He still loves us with His all, even when we become bitter and rebellious after suffering the consequences of our actions. Some resort to blaming God, asking, *"Why me?"* or saying, *"I guess God doesn't care about me..."* God blessed us when He created us, for He placed His values within us and made us in His image.

A minister friend of mine, Patti Pena, made a social media post about our fruits

"The Lord shall fight for you, and ye shall hold your peace." (KJV) Exodus 14:14

becoming bitter and resentful because of our pasts. Our fruits wither and dry because they are not being nurtured spiritually.

Is this not what happens to children when they do not receive the love, care and attention they need from their parents?

We are God's children; we are His Kings and Queens, having been perfected through Him and by Him. God didn't just make us, he created us inside and out. How, then, could His Spirit not know what we

"The Lord shall fight for you, and ye shall hold your peace." (KJV) Exodus 14:14

need, or how to intercede when we need it

the most?

John 14:16

"And I will pray the Father, and he shall give you another Comforter, that He may abide with you forever."

Which locusts are preventing the

Power of the Holy Spirit from working

through you and shining from within others?

Ask yourself: are you tired of being

devoured? If so, are you ready to be set free?

"The Lord shall fight for you, and ye shall hold your peace." (KJV) Exodus 14:14

Ephesians 4:30

"And do not make God's Holy Spirit sad; for the Spirit is God's mark of ownership on you, a guarantee that the Day will come when God will set you free."

The Holy Spirit cannot be restrained, but it can be hindered and rejected.

It is because we do evil things against the Holy Spirit that our eternal position in Heaven, which God has already promised us, is now at risk. Those who serve worldly things must know this: those things are not

"The Lord shall fight for you, and ye shall hold your peace." (KJV) Exodus 14:14

eternal, and neither is our flesh. It, like every other living thing, will grow old, wither and die.

Locusts can only devour us completely with our permission. Serpents cannot enter our territory or environment without our consent. They will keep us in darkness and in bondage only if we permit it.

Remember: it is by the *Power of the Holy Spirit* and by *faith* that we can and are set free from those places which are without light. Darkness is not a place of God; rather,

"The Lord shall fight for you, and ye shall hold your peace." (KJV) Exodus 14:14

it is a place of torment which hinders the spirits of peace, joy, and love. These spirits are also hindered when one continues to focus on the number, size and speed of the of the locusts which we encounter.

James 2:26

"So then, as the body without the spirit is dead, so also faith without actions is dead."

Once we focus on the locusts, fear takes over our spirits, and with fear comes actions

"The Lord shall fight for you, and ye shall hold your peace." (KJV) Exodus 14:14

steeped in unnecessary risks. The result is that our spirits are plunged into poverty.

Personal Reflection:

Do you now understand how the Power of the Holy Spirit may be hindered?

Are you willing to learn more about the Power of the Holy Spirit and how it can take root in your life?

Do you understand that Jesus Christ is the Way, the Truth, the Light, and our means to spiritual freedom?

"The Lord shall fight for you, and ye shall hold your peace." (KJV) Exodus 14:14

Are you willing to learn and understand more about how and why Jesus Christ is our means to spiritual freedom?

Take the time to pray to God. Ask for guidance, wisdom, and understanding based on the answers you provide.

"The Lord shall fight for you, and ye shall hold your peace." (KJV) Exodus 14:14

Chapter 5: The Spirit or The Locust

As you read this book, ask yourself: what stage has your life reached? Are you allowing the *Spirit of God* to subdue you, or are your locusts attacking every branch of your tree? One thing I have learned on my journey and during my career is that locusts either attack our mental state first, which manifests itself physically; or they begin with our physical state, which manifests itself mentally. Therefore, God yearns for His People to hear and seek comfort in His Voice.

"The Lord shall fight for you, and ye shall hold your peace." (KJV) Exodus 14:14

God's door is always open, and His Words call us to Him, but many are still controlled by their fellow man, material things, and evil spirits. We as humans have a natural inclination to attempt to restore the goodness of our fruits on our own. God intends for every fruit our garden holds (whether it's our finances, wife, children, siblings, parents, job, and love), to prosper.

Matthew 12:33

"Either make the tree good, and his fruit good; or else make the tree corrupt, and his fruit corrupt: for the tree is known by his fruit."

"The Lord shall fight for you, and ye shall hold your peace." (KJV) Exodus 14:14

It is not possible for a fruit tree or a garden to be spiritually replenished without *God's Word* and the intercession of *His Holy Spirit.* It is by and through the *Power of the Holy Spirit* that we experience restoration, deliverance, nurturing, which causes our sinful natures to wither and die. Locusts can no longer survive; as your spirit is being fed by God, they starve. Serpents can no longer slither their way into your life; they cannot withstand the Flame of the Holy Spirit.

"The Lord shall fight for you, and ye shall hold your peace." (KJV) Exodus 14:14

We as individuals have the power to determine whether we will live as directed by our flesh and by society, or in accordance with God's Word and Will. *God's Holy Spirit* and locusts do not now occupy, nor will they ever occupy, the same space; what they each bring with their presence is vastly different. Locusts bring fear, natural disaster, human misery, and destruction. The Holy Spirit, however, brings God's Eternal Love and Breath of Life, together with actions and attitudes of faith, nurturing, and good fruits that will multiply in perpetuity.

"The Lord shall fight for you, and ye shall hold your peace." (KJV) Exodus 14:14

One can either adhere to the Holy Spirit or adhere to the whim and fancies of locusts and serpents. With that in mind, I ask you this: are you living with the *Holy Spirit,* or with the locusts? Are you living with the Holy Spirit, or are your serpents getting bigger and more powerful every day? Which power or influence are you choosing to feed today? Some of us can stop what we are doing, right now, and lay our life down for Christ. God wants to lead us out of the darkness, so that we may be given a life covered in His Light.

"The Lord shall fight for you, and ye shall hold your peace." (KJV) Exodus 14:14

2 Corinthians 3:8

"For the Spirit gives life."

To be honest, many people will not answer God's Call to us until they ready to do so. There are also those who believe that they are not ready, but God knows different. God allows us to suffer from the consequences of our disobedience, so that we may receive Him and His Attention.

God never gives up on His Children; He never stops leading us, instructing us, or believing in us.

"The Lord shall fight for you, and ye shall hold your peace." (KJV) Exodus 14:14

In a similar fashion, locusts will never stop devouring God's Children until we surrender ourselves and the locusts to God, and until we listen to and obey the directions of ***His Holy Spirit***. The ***Spirit of God*** does not lie, nor can it lie, and God Himself has promised us an eternal resting place after this life is finished.

Titus 1:2

"In hope of eternal life, which God, that cannot lie, promised before the world began."

"The Lord shall fight for you, and ye shall hold your peace." (KJV) Exodus 14:14

Why would God promise us such a thing if he could not or would not deliver it? Why would God make such a promise if He was not completely concerned about us?

God's Word is truly inspirational, and it outlines the absolute truth regarding how we should live our lives. God's Word provides us counsel for our problems, mentors our character, intercedes on our behalf, increases our spiritual maturity, and builds a firm spiritual foundation within us.

"The Lord shall fight for you, and ye shall hold your peace." (KJV) Exodus 14:14

God created us to love, listen to and follow His Will so that we will not only serve His Purpose for His Glory, but so we can also live in our greater. As a witness to God's Providence with several testimonies, I must admit that I love living in my greater. I am of flesh, just like you, so there are times when locusts still try to attack me, and when the serpents still try to enter my territory, but by God's Grace, I will never open my door to them again.

"The Lord shall fight for you, and ye shall hold your peace." (KJV) Exodus 14:14

You are just as capable of releasing the locusts and serpents from your life as I am. With that in mind, what will it be: The *Holy Spirit*, or the locusts and serpents?

Personal Reflection:

This may take a while to consider, depending on what stage in life you are in: if you have not already, will you choose God today and follow His Holy Spirit?

Reflect on one of the more difficult situations in your life that caused you to suffer from the consequences of your actions or omissions.

"The Lord shall fight for you, and ye shall hold your peace." (KJV) Exodus 14:14

How did you escape? Once you escaped, how did your freedom feel?

Are there any other steps which you are willing to take to bring an end to your suffering?

Take the time to pray to God and ask Him for guidance in these important matters.

"The Lord shall fight for you, and ye shall hold your peace." (KJV) Exodus 14:14

Chapter 6: Body of Christ

Romans 8:10

"And if Christ be in you, the body is dead because of sin; but the Spirit is life because of righteousness."

The **Body of Christ** has no room for evildoers, false prophets, liars, or any other thing which is contrary to God's Teachings and His Truth. The Scripture from James 4:7 instructs us to submit ourselves to God, resisting the devil, and the devil will flee. According to Philippians 4:13, *"we can do all things through Christ who strengthens us."*

"The Lord shall fight for you, and ye shall hold your peace." (KJV) Exodus 14:14

The ***Body of Christ*** comprises of prayer warriors, believers, teachers of truth, leaders of love and wisdom, and the communities we live in or are otherwise a part of. The membership of the True Body of Christ does not infight, nor does it seek to tear its individual members down; instead, they help fight off the locusts and serpents with the aid of God's Word, Inspiration, and Encouragement.

God's Word is the one and only true sword which we can carry everywhere we go.

"The Lord shall fight for you, and ye shall hold your peace." (KJV) Exodus 14:14

We can read it, speak it, write it, text it, teach with it, pray with it, sing it, hang it on our walls, travel with it, and allow it to manifest it our hearts. The true **Body of Christ** will always triumph over the locusts and serpents in the end; victory is God's, and God's alone.

My testimony (Part 3)

I can recall returning home from work around 7:00 p.m. or 8:00 p.m. one day. I walked through the door and placed my work bags on the kitchen counter top.

"The Lord shall fight for you, and ye shall hold your peace." (KJV) Exodus 14:14

I stopped to take a long look around my home. My spirit was uneasy spirit, my heart was confused, and my mind was exhausted.

My work bags were filled with the work I needed to complete. My homework was in the corner of my living room, waiting to be completed. My son was in his room watching television, anticipating his afternoon hug and bath. My daughter was finishing her homework and waiting for dinner. Unpacked boxes filled almost every room in the house.

"The Lord shall fight for you, and ye shall hold your peace." (KJV) Exodus 14:14

The laundry was arranged in seemingly endless piles. The kitchen was in an offensively untidy state. Our Labrador was standing in front of me, with a quizzical look on its face, almost as if to ask, *"What's wrong?"* My bills were piling up. All in all, I was disgusted with myself.

I was running back and forth to therapy with and for my son.

"The Lord shall fight for you, and ye shall hold your peace." (KJV) Exodus 14:14

In addition, I was working full time, attending school full time, keeping up with my daughter's activities, handling gossip from other parents to the effect that I was never there for my daughter (or that I was late when I was), contemplating leaving a toxic relationship, digesting all the things my son was going through and had yet to go through, and I just felt overwhelmed by it all. I worked tirelessly, every single day, to help others to the best of my ability. In that moment, I considered the possibility that ensuring my children's happiness would cost me my own.

"The Lord shall fight for you, and ye shall hold your peace." (KJV) Exodus 14:14

I felt like I was forgotten; like no one truly understood that I needed help. My son had so many problems and appointments, and I was the only adult in his life to make sure that they were adequately taken care of. His sister was so angry about her broken relationship with the only father she'd ever truly known, that she required counseling. She was being picked on and bullied at school about her brother's special needs. She was going through the motions, asking God why He would make her brother 'that way,' knowing she always wanted a sibling.

"The Lord shall fight for you, and ye shall hold your peace." (KJV) Exodus 14:14

My daughter knew how to hide her anger from the world. In the meantime, I started a new relationship because it had everything the old one did not, and I allowed myself to fall deeply into it. I was being devoured by all those things, at once. I allowed darkness to take root in my life, take over, and settle in. I remember telling God that I just couldn't take it anymore. It did not matter how good of a job I was doing at work, how wonderful a mother people thought I was, or how well I was performing at school.

"The Lord shall fight for you, and ye shall hold your peace." (KJV) Exodus 14:14

I was done with my life and equally done with all its afflictions and challenges. I no longer wanted to process any feelings, emotions, or situations. With that, I set what I thought was my final plan into motion.

Once my children were in their beds, I looked around my home one last time and kissed my children goodnight. I knew that would be my last earthly kiss for them. I went into my restroom for an evening soak and prepared for what was about to take place. I wrote a letter and placed it away from the bathroom, so that it would not get wet.

"The Lord shall fight for you, and ye shall hold your peace." (KJV) Exodus 14:14

The letter contained my apologies, together with directions and instructions for my children. I climbed in the bathtub and took the battery out of my cell phone. I started crying, and I asked God for forgiveness. I was emotionally and mentally drained. I laid back and took about five extra - strength sleeping pills. After about five minutes, I decided they were not working fast enough.

My coworker sent me a message about one of my clients because I was on a call with

"The Lord shall fight for you, and ye shall hold your peace." (KJV) Exodus 14:14

another phone. By this time, I had taken another ten pills.

I took the battery out of the phone and threw it across the floor. In my own anger and disgust, I thought about the type of mother who leaves her children to fend for themselves, after which I took another ten sleeping pills. I kept taking sleeping pills until there were only about 3 or 4 out of a 60 – count bottle. I began losing consciousness.

Shortly afterwards, I heard my Labrador barking so loudly that I was unable

"The Lord shall fight for you, and ye shall hold your peace." (KJV) Exodus 14:14

to completely lose consciousness. I also heard loud knocks on the door and other dogs barking loudly.

My only other memory of that incident was of someone lifting me out of the bathtub. I barely remember seeing my Labrador with one of the responders. I lost consciousness just as I was being lifted out of the bathtub. I eventually regained consciousness to a doctor asking me questions. It took everything in me just to whisper nonsense, like a two or three - year old, then I lost consciousness once again.

"The Lord shall fight for you, and ye shall hold your peace." (KJV) Exodus 14:14

This is the first time since February 2012 that I have explained those circumstances in this manner.

This story has so much more to it than I have revealed. This may not be the end of my testimony, but the most important thing is that God did what the doctors could not do. He saved my life and brought me into a new purpose, a new destiny, and a stronger, unexplainable relationship with Him. The doctors could not figure out how I survived, experienced no brain damage, and did not require any extensive therapy or treatment

"The Lord shall fight for you, and ye shall hold your peace." (KJV) Exodus 14:14

during my periods of recuperation. During this entire ordeal, I returned to my first love: my Lord and Savior Jesus Christ.

I sought God for His Directions and His Will. I prayed to God and asked Him to remove me from the things and people I allowed to hold me in bondage. God did more than that in answering my prayer: He granted me the power and wisdom to achieve victory through His *Holy Spirit.*

If you are reading this and feel like your locusts and serpents have taken you to a

"The Lord shall fight for you, and ye shall hold your peace." (KJV) Exodus 14:14

place beyond redemption, I am here to tell you, as a witness to God's Greatness, that the devil is a liar.

"The Lord shall fight for you, and ye shall hold your peace." (KJV) Exodus 14:14

God has in fact designed a divine purpose for you and your life; after all, your body is His Temple, first and foremost. Your thoughts are not God's Thoughts, and your ways are not His Ways. The thoughts described in my testimony were mine and mine alone; they were not Fruits of the Holy Spirit. My old ways were neither the Ways nor the Will of God. God kept His promise to me and revealed a greater purpose for my life than its premature end by my own hands.

"The Lord shall fight for you, and ye shall hold your peace." (KJV) Exodus 14:14

Isaiah 55:8

"For my thoughts are not your thoughts, neither are your ways my ways, saith the LORD."

God is our truth, love, peace, and perfect partner in prayer. He removes the locusts and serpents in our lives by saving us and drawing us closer to Him. Our spirits must be restored and renewed in Christ, so that we will no longer falter in the enemy's presence.

"The Lord shall fight for you, and ye shall hold your peace." (KJV) Exodus 14:14

Carrying the Sword of Christ on the inside of us protects us externally, because God's Word penetrates and manifests over our flesh.

Though it was not difficult for me to write my testimony, it still evoked tears. These were tears not of sadness, but of gratitude. I am forever grateful to God that He saved me for a greater purpose. My testimony did not end where I left it, as God took His Time in removing all the locusts and serpents from my life, and in evacuating me from darkness.

"The Lord shall fight for you, and ye shall hold your peace." (KJV) Exodus 14:14

God already knows and understands that this process is not immediate. It is this lack of immediacy that causes us to hesitate in undergoing it. Always remember that our thoughts are not His Thoughts, and that our God is a God of forgiveness.

You may think, as I used to, that your life is worthless. It is when the storm is at its fiercest and most calamitous that we spiritually mature the most, and with that maturity, determine whether we will either submit to the storm, or conquer it, with the

"The Lord shall fight for you, and ye shall hold your peace." (KJV) Exodus 14:14

understanding that we belong to the ***Body of Christ***.

Just because we all tend to have bad seasons, doesn't mean we cannot bear good fruit while those bad seasons last. No matter what season we are in, we must constantly be reminded of God's Word. We must keep close to Him and pray often.

Make no mistake: God will give locusts temporary permission to test our faith and the strength of the ***Body of Christ*** which dwells within us. No locust or serpent can

"The Lord shall fight for you, and ye shall hold your peace." (KJV) Exodus 14:14

follow us to our final resting place, which

God has already promised.

"The Lord shall fight for you, and ye shall hold your peace." (KJV) Exodus 14:14

God leads us towards heavenly things within His purpose that are music to our ears and food to our spirit. How annoying is the sound locusts make when they attack, and the devastation they leave behind? How chaotic and confusing is it dealing with serpents whose only goal is to kill, steal and destroy? We stubbornly continue to make our own decisions, even though God has said:

"The Lord shall fight for you, and ye shall hold your peace." (KJV) Exodus 14:14

John 14:6

"Jesus saith unto him, I am the way, the truth, and the life: no man cometh unto the Father, but by me."

Luke 6:46

"And why call ye me, Lord, Lord, and do not the things which I say?"

It bears repeating that it is because we continue to do things our way that locusts can devour us. Our space, our time, and our hearts are the three primary things we ought to sacrifice for Christ, which in turn will prevent locusts from devouring us, and by extension, hindering the ***Holy Spirit*** and our blessings which are to come our way.

"The Lord shall fight for you, and ye shall hold your peace." (KJV) Exodus 14:14

We became God's Blessing in the beginning when He created us. The Scripture informs us that God knew us before we were formed in the womb (Jeremiah 1:5). We serve a mighty God; when He is for us, He can obliterate anything or anyone which stands against us. God gave His Only Begotten Son to us, so that we will be saved for His Glory and Purpose. What a great purpose God has designed for each person He has made in the likeness of His image!

"The Lord shall fight for you, and ye shall hold your peace." (KJV) Exodus 14:14

God loves us so much that He will never leave or forsake us. We, first and foremost, belong to the **Body of Christ.** Locusts, on the other hand, will devour us, placing us in the position for bondage and destruction, thereby opening the door for serpents as well. God will not destroy us in the process of destroying the enemy; but we will undoubtedly suffer the consequences of our own actions.

"The Lord shall fight for you, and ye shall hold your peace." (KJV) Exodus 14:14

Know that the ministry family and I are praying for your release and deliverance. There is absolutely nothing that God cannot handle, and we love you from the bottom of our hearts.

Romans 12:5

"So we, being many, are one body in Christ, and every one members one of another."

Personal Reflection:

What situation(s) are you holding on to?

Are you willing to turn that situation over to Christ and allow Him to operate on it?

"The Lord shall fight for you, and ye shall hold your peace." (KJV) Exodus 14:14

Do you understand that you are a Body of Christ and the significance of that fact?

Having read Chapters 3 – 6, what noteworthy steps are you willing to take to function as the Vessel of God that you are?

Take the time to pray to God and ask Him about turning your life over to Him, and what steps you must take to work for Him.

"The Lord shall fight for you, and ye shall hold your peace." (KJV) Exodus 14:14

Chapter 7: Spiritual Completion

'Complete' is defined as *'having all parts or elements; lacking nothing; whole; entire; full.'* Jesus Christ helps us reach our destinations, conquers our trials, and calms the storms in our lives, but there is more to it.

God has promised us eternity in a place that we can only enter through Jesus Christ. God desires for us to have a brand new and unexplainable joy in our lives.

"The Lord shall fight for you, and ye shall hold your peace." (KJV) Exodus 14:14

God takes every trial and tribulation and brews it into something new and complete. One of the joys I can sing about right now is being able to work from my home office, from which I can complete my God – given assignments. I never thought this would happen in my life, nor did I imagine that it was something God had in store for me. Everything I do from home currently is for the ministry and for helping others.

"The Lord shall fight for you, and ye shall hold your peace." (KJV) Exodus 14:14

My locusts in the beginning of this process were: taking my time for granted; complaining about not having a full - time job with a guaranteed pay check and being angry about my status as a housewife. God was the only One who could continue revealing this process and its importance to me.

Let's take another look at the titles in this book, because the titles consist of steps for each of us:

"The Lord shall fight for you, and ye shall hold your peace." (KJV) Exodus 14:14

^ Give the locust to Christ (submit)

^ Follow God's Directions (obedience)

^ Step out on Faith (trust)

^ Stop Hindering Spiritual Gifts (Holy Spirit)

^ Increase Spiritual Maturity (wisdom)

^ One is God's Vessel (Body of Christ)

^ We all have a Season (Spiritual Completion)

"The Lord shall fight for you, and ye shall hold your peace." (KJV) Exodus 14:14

The more we overcome our locusts, the more spiritually prepared we become. Once we are prepared in our spirits, our fruits will start to blossom unlike anything we have ever witnessed before; our seasons are sprinkled with prosperity; and our hearts begin to appreciate God's Blessings more. Our spiritual maturity operates out of wisdom and inner prompts from the Holy Spirit. We long to deal directly with Christ to reach our full spiritual completion.

"The Lord shall fight for you, and ye shall hold your peace." (KJV) Exodus 14:14

Acts 2:28

"Thou hast made known to me the ways of life; thou shalt make me full of joy with thy countenance."

Ultimately, locusts and serpents are not what God has in store for us; for they do not give life, but rather, they take it away through suffocation. We are individually responsible for our spiritual welfare. God is looking for us to accept the commission He has given. He brings our spiritual completion to pass and leads us to the eternal resting place He has already promised.

"The Lord shall fight for you, and ye shall hold your peace." (KJV) Exodus 14:14

I want to encourage you as I have been encouraged through the wisdom of Christ to fire your flesh, put on your new, and complete your spiritual journey.

Personal Reflection:

Briefly reflect on the questions asked in Chapters 1 – 6:

List at least two to three things you learned from each chapter.

What changes (if any) have you made after reading each chapter?

> *"The Lord shall fight for you, and ye shall hold your peace."* (KJV) Exodus 14:14

Name at least three things you are certain will be different, having read this book.

Did you take time to pray after each chapter? Be honest.

If you prayed, did it help you increase the quality of your prayer life?

Take the time to pray to God without any distractions. Write a journal about how what you have read in this book has made you feel.

"The Lord shall fight for you, and ye shall hold your peace." (KJV) Exodus 14:14

Authors Scripture Selection

EXODUS 14:14

"THE LORD SHALL FIGHT FOR YOU, AND YE SHALL HOLD YOUR PEACE."

EXODUS 10:15

"FOR THEY COVERED THE FACE OF THE WHOLE EARTH, SO THAT THE LAND WAS DARKENED; AND THEY DID EAT EVERY HERB OF THE LAND, AND ALL THE FRUIT OF THE TREES WHICH THE HAIL HAD LEFT: AND THERE REMAINED NOT ANY GREEN THING IN THE TREES, OR IN THE HERBS OF THE FIELD..."

DEUTERONOMY 28:42

"ALL THY TREES AND FRUIT OF THY LAND SHALL THE LOCUST CONSUME."

PROVERBS 2:6

"FOR THE LORD GIVES WISDOM; FROM HIS MOUTH COME KNOWLEDGE AND UNDERSTANDING."

PROVERBS 30:27

"THE LOCUSTS HAVE NO KING, YET THEY ALL ADVANCE IN RANKS."

"The Lord shall fight for you, and ye shall hold your peace." (KJV) Exodus 14:14

JEREMIAH 29:11

"FOR I KNOW THE THOUGHTS I THINK TOWARDS YOU, SAYS THE LORD, THOUGHTS OF PEACE AND NOT OF EVIL, TO GIVE YOU A FUTURE AND A HOPE."

JOHN 8:32

"AND YE SHALL KNOW THE TRUTH, AND THE TRUTH SHALL MAKE YOU FREE."

PROVERBS 1:7

"THE FEAR OF THE LORD IS THE BEGINNING OF KNOWLEDGE: BUT FOOLS DESPISE WISDOM AND INSTRUCTION."

PROVERBS 3:5

"TRUST IN THE LORD WITH ALL THINE HEART; AND LEAN NOT UNTO THINE OWN UNDERSTANDING."

TITUS 1:2

"IN HOPE OF ETERNAL LIFE, WHICH GOD, THAT CANNOT LIE, PROMISED BEFORE THE WORLD BEGAN."

1 JOHN 4:1

"BELOVED, BELIEVE NOT EVERY SPIRIT, BUT TRY THE SPIRITS WHETHER THEY ARE OF GOD: BECAUSE MANY FALSE PROPHETS ARE GONE OUT INTO THE WORLD."

"The Lord shall fight for you, and ye shall hold your peace." (KJV) Exodus 14:14

JOHN 14:16

"AND I WILL PRAY THE FATHER, AND HE SHALL GIVE YOU ANOTHER COMFORTER, THAT HE MAY ABIDE WITH YOU FOREVER."

EPHESIANS 4:30

"AND DO NOT MAKE GOD'S HOLY SPIRIT SAD; FOR THE SPIRIT IS GOD'S MARK OF OWNERSHIP ON YOU, A GUARANTEE THAT THE DAY WILL COME WHEN GOD WILL SET YOU FREE."

JAMES 2:26

"SO THEN, AS THE BODY WITHOUT THE SPIRIT IS DEAD, SO ALSO FAITH WITHOUT ACTIONS IS DEAD."

MATTHEW 12:33

"EITHER MAKE THE TREE GOOD, AND HIS FRUIT GOOD; OR ELSE MAKE THE TREE CORRUPT, AND HIS FRUIT CORRUPT: FOR THE TREE IS KNOWN BY HIS FRUIT."

2 CORINTHIANS 3:8

"FOR THE SPIRIT GIVES LIFE."

TITUS 1:2

"IN HOPE OF ETERNAL LIFE, WHICH GOD, THAT CANNOT LIE, PROMISED BEFORE THE WORLD BEGAN."

"The Lord shall fight for you, and ye shall hold your peace." (KJV) Exodus 14:14

ROMANS 8:10

"AND IF CHRIST BE IN YOU, THE BODY IS DEAD BECAUSE OF SIN; BUT THE SPIRIT IS LIFE BECAUSE OF RIGHTEOUSNESS."

ISAIAH 55:8

"FOR MY THOUGHTS ARE NOT YOUR THOUGHTS, NEITHER ARE YOUR WAYS MY WAYS, SAITH THE LORD."

JOHN 14:6

"JESUS SAITH UNTO HIM, I AM THE WAY, THE TRUTH, AND THE LIFE: NO MAN COMETH UNTO THE FATHER, BUT BY ME."

LUKE 6:46

"AND WHY CALL YE ME, LORD, LORD, AND DO NOT THE THINGS WHICH I SAY?"

ROMANS 12:5

"SO WE, BEING MANY, ARE ONE BODY IN CHRIST, AND EVERY ONE MEMBERS ONE OF ANOTHER."

ACTS 2:28

"THOU HAST MADE KNOWN TO ME THE WAYS OF LIFE; THOU SHALT MAKE ME FULL OF JOY WITH THY COUNTENANCE."

"The Lord shall fight for you, and ye shall hold your peace." (KJV) Exodus 14:14

Scriptures for A Journey

Proverbs 3:6

"In all thy ways acknowledge him, and he shall direct thy paths."

Jeremiah 17:7

"Blessed is the man that trusteth in the Lord, and whose hope the Lord is."

Philippians 1:6

"Being confident of this very thing, that he which hath begun a good work in you will perform it until the day of Jesus Christ."

Colossians 2:6-7

"As ye have therefore received Christ Jesus the Lord, so walk ye in him: Rooted and built up in him, and stablished in the faith, as ye have been taught, abounding therein with thanksgiving."

"The Lord shall fight for you, and ye shall hold your peace." (KJV) Exodus 14:14

James 1:4-5

"But let patience have her perfect work, that ye may be perfect and entire, wanting nothing. If any of you lack wisdom, let him ask of God, that giveth all men liberally, and upbraideth not; and it shall be given him."

"The Lord shall fight for you, and ye shall hold your peace." (KJV) Exodus 14:14

Follow Us:

God Simple Solutions Ministry Group

https://www.facebook.com/groups/79842872365087
7/

New Level Inspirations Promised Covenant Page

https://www.facebook.com/inspiredbyChrist/

Shop De'Christian Store

*https://www.facebook.com/DeChristian-
134190047269172/*

Instagram

*Shop_dechristian7_*

*"The Lord shall fight for you, and ye shall hold your
peace."* (KJV) Exodus 14:14

Made in the USA
Middletown, DE
15 February 2018